JD's Superhero Day at Home
Fighting Baddy Germs

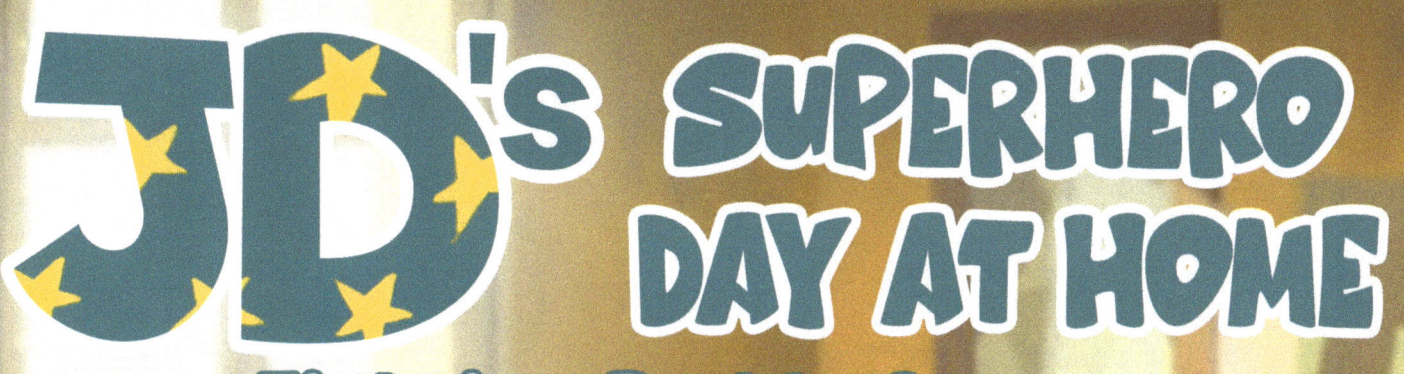

Angeles Fisher

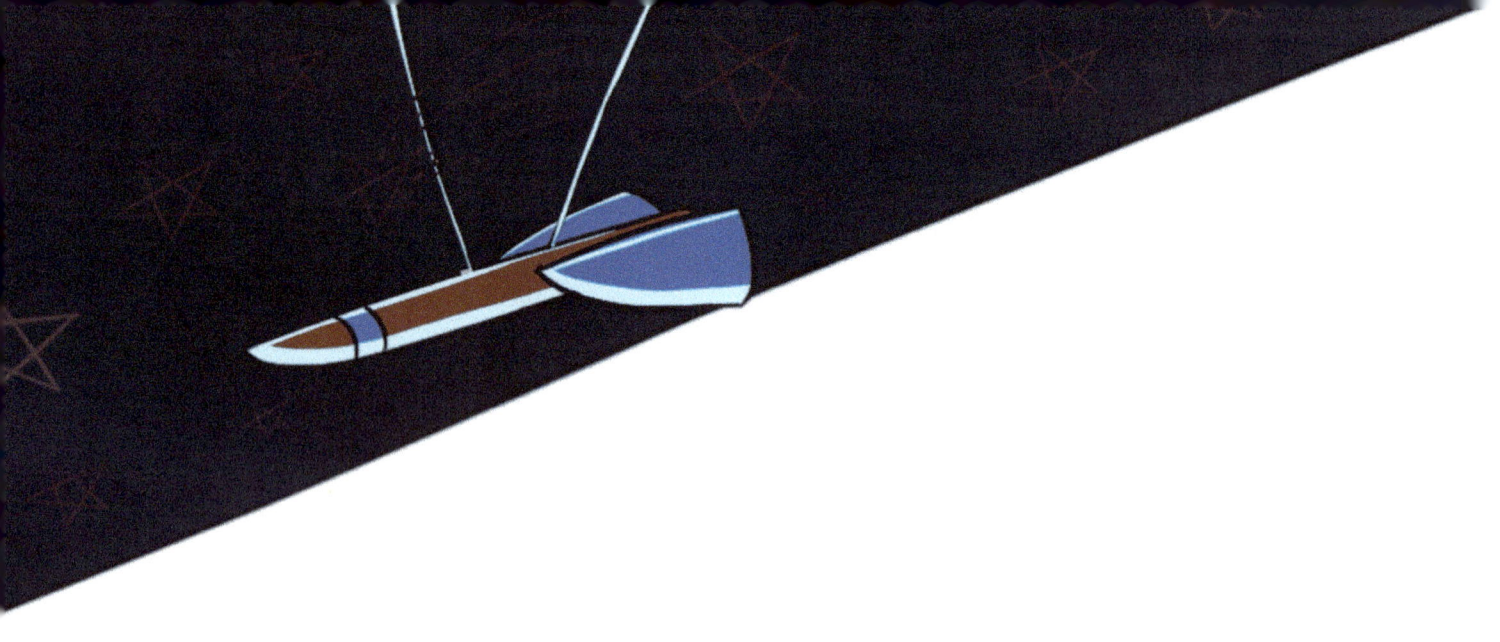

JD's Superhero Day at Home
Copyright © 2020 by Angeles Fisher

All rights reserved. No part of this publication may be reproduced, distributed, or transmitted in any form or by any means, including photocopying, recording, or other electronic or mechanical methods, without the prior written permission of the author, except in the case of brief quotations embodied in critical reviews and certain other non-commercial uses permitted by copyright law.

Tellwell Talent
www.tellwell.ca

ISBN
978-0-2288-3222-5 (Hardcover)
978-0-2288-3221-8 (Paperback)
978-0-2288-3223-2 (eBook)

I dedicate this book to Daniel, Jaden, Leneah and Skyler Fisher, my dear family. I wrote this as a memory of the hard times for us and the whole world, and as a reminder that family is and always will be the most important thing in life.

I also dedicate this book to all the heroes that saved the world in 2020.

"Mom, look at our costumes. We're superheroes!" yelled JD.

"Wow!" said Mom.

"You three look fantastic!" said Dad.

"Can I go out to show my friends?" JD asked.

"We can't leave the house," said Mom, sadly. "You and Nea have colds."

"Oh! Why can't we visit our friends when we have colds?" asked JD.

"How can we be superheroes if we can't go out?" asked Nea.

"Well," said Dad, "You can fight a whole army of invisible baddies right here."

"Who?" asked JD. "I can't see any invisible baddies."

"That's because they're invisible!" said Mom. "They're tiny germs that make people feel yucky. You don't want to give your cold germs to anyone else, do you?"

"What are germs?" asked Nea.

"Germs are very tiny bugs that cause diseases. They are so tiny that they can only be seen through a microscope," said Mom.

"If you stay in," said Dad, "you'll beat them by washing your hands a lot and covering your face when you sneeze and cough. You might even save lives, just like firefighters do."

"And doctors?" asked JD.

"And nurses?" asked Nea.

"Exactly!" said Dad. "The doctor said you just have the sniffles, but it is best to stay home until you get better."

"The baddies can't beat superheroes like you. But you could pass them to someone who's already feeling sick. It could be dangerous," said Mom.

"You're right!" said JD. "I'll keep my cold away from my friends. Superheroes need to be CARING about other people."

"I know what we'll do," said Mom. "Let's make some cool masks for your costumes."

JD and Nea made wonderful masks and helped Sky with his.

"Thank you for helping Sky," said Mom. "Superheroes are always KIND."

After they finished, Nea said she wanted to see Grandpa and Grandma.

"Yes!" shouted JD. He was very excited. "They'll love our costumes!"

"Do you kids think it's a good idea to visit your grandparents when you have a cold?" asked Mom.

"What if they catch your cold?" asked Dad.

"Elders in our community aren't as strong as superheroes like you. They need a superhero to fight the baddie germs" explained Dad.

"We'll be BRAVE and STRONG for them," said JD. "We'll stay home and fight the baddie bugs."

JD raised his arm and ran around the room like Superman. Then he sneezed.

Nea ran around as well. Then she coughed.

Sky tried to run around but fell over and started giggling.

"Mom!" cried JD, suddenly. "I've got a great idea. Can we send Grandma and Grandpa a special bat signal?"

"A what?" asked Mom.

"We can still show them our costumes on a video call. That's how people talk to Batman. They send a bat signal."

"Great idea!" said Mom. "You're as CLEVER as Batman and Spiderman and all the other superheroes."

Mom told the children to wash their hands before touching the computer.

"Why?" asked Nea. "My hands aren't dirty."

"The baddies love hiding on your hands," said Mom. "Then they spread to whatever you touch."

"Dad and I don't have colds. Washing your hands will help keep us safe. Superheroes need to be CAREFUL."

The children rushed to the sink.
"Here's a song to sing while washing your hands," said Mom.

Germs are invisible,
your nose is irresistible.
They'll get inside with ease,
so, don't let them be a tease!

We are superheroes!
We will beat germs!

Germs can spread
when you touch your face.
If you scrub your hands,
those germs will be erased.

We are superheroes!
We will beat germs!

Healthy food will make us strong,
so we can play all day long!
Scrubbing our hands is key
to our health and safety!

"Take that, baddies!" sang JD as he washed his hands.
"Get lost, germs!" cried Nea.

That evening, Mom put the children to bed. "I'm sorry you had to stay in," she said.

"Why?" said JD. "I've had an awesome day. I learned all about superheroes. I found out they are BRAVE, KIND, STRONG, CARING, CLEVER and CAREFUL."

"Just like you," smiled Mom.

"I saved lots of people from getting sick, as well. Then, I beat an army of invisible baddies with the Handwashing Song!"

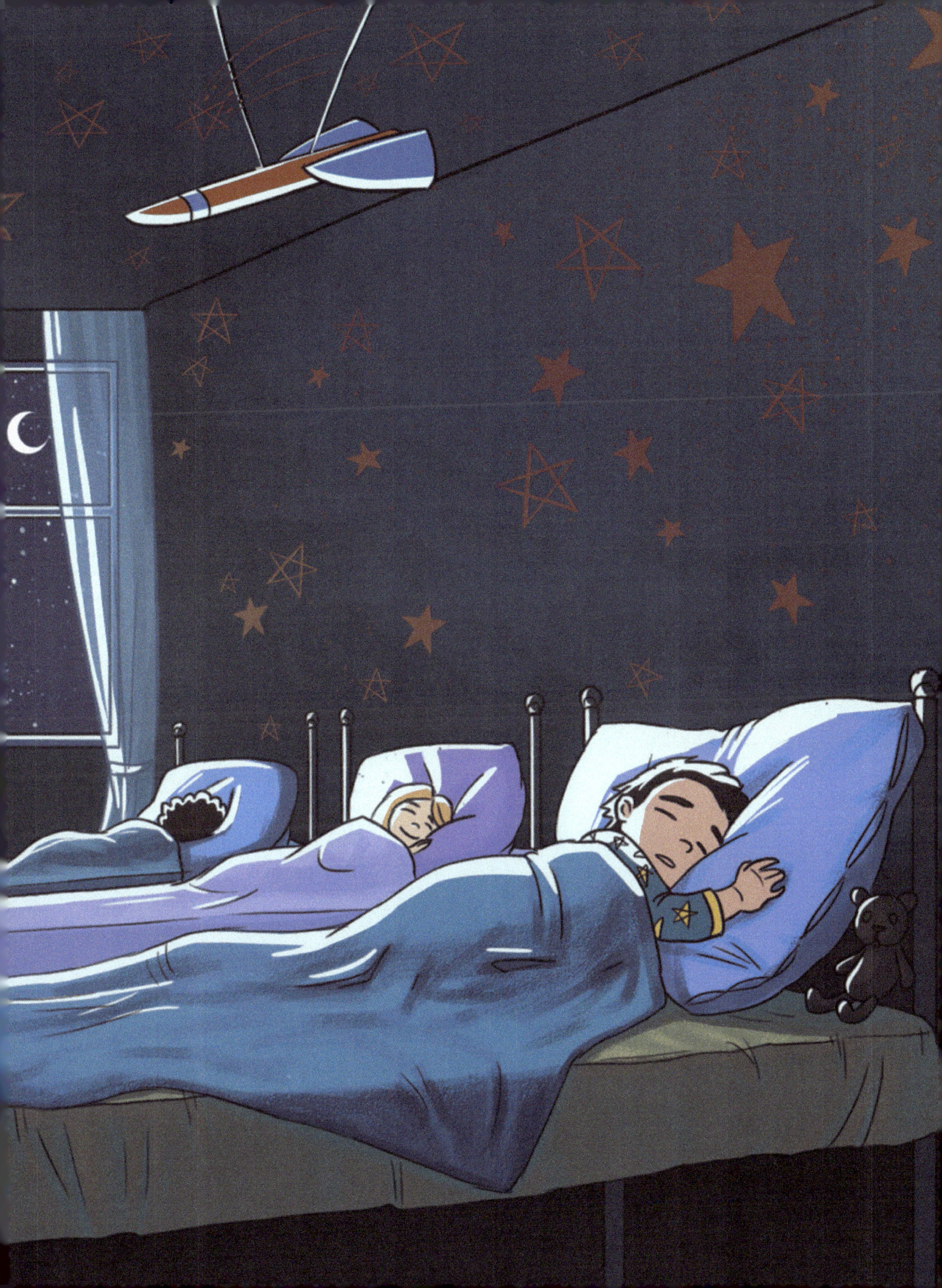

"Goodnight, Mom."

JD yawned. He was very tired. It was hard work being a superhero.

www.ingramcontent.com/pod-product-compliance
Lightning Source LLC
LaVergne TN
LVHW072051060526
838200LV00061B/4711